HAL•LEONARD

JAZZ PLAY-ALONG®

Book and CD for B♭, E♭, C and Bass Clef Instruments

Volume 135

Arranged and Produced by Mark Taylor

JEFF BECK

BOOK

CD

Cover photo © Marty Temme

ISBN 978-1-4234-9447-8

HAL•LEONARD®
CORPORATION
7777 W. BLUEMOUND RD. P.O. BOX 13819 MILWAUKEE, WI 53213

Visit Hal Leonard Online at
www.halleonard.com

D0584766

JEFF BECK

Volume 135

Arranged and Produced by
Mark Taylor

Featured Players:

Paul Murtha–Trumpet
John Desalme–Sax
Tony Nalker–Piano
Jim Roberts–Bass/Guitar
Todd Harrison–Drums

Recorded at Bias Studios, Springfield, Virginia
Bob Dawson, Engineer

HOW TO USE THE CD:

Each song has <u>two</u> tracks:

1) Split Track/Melody

Woodwind, Brass, Keyboard, and **Mallet Players** can use this track as a learning tool for melody style and inflection.

Bass Players can learn and perform with this track – remove the recorded bass track by turning down the volume on the LEFT channel.

Keyboard and **Guitar Players** can learn and perform with this track – remove the recorded piano part by turning down the volume on the RIGHT channel.

2) Full Stereo Track

Soloists or **Groups** can learn and perform with this accompaniment track with the RHYTHM SECTION only.

CD

1 : SPLIT TRACK/MELODY
2 : FULL STEREO TRACK

BLUE WIND

BY JAN HAMMER

C VERSION

SOLOS (3 CHORUSES)

D.S. AL CODA

⊕ CODA

BASS

Cause We've Ended as Lovers

CD
③ : SPLIT TRACK/MELODY
④ : FULL STEREO TRACK

WORDS AND MUSIC BY
STEVIE WONDER

C VERSION

SLOW ROCK BALLAD

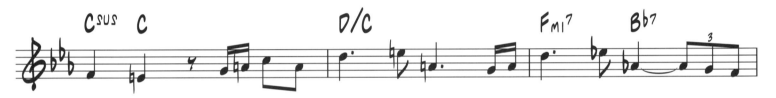

FREEWAY JAM

BY MAX MIDDLETON

CD
◆ 7 : SPLIT TRACK/MELODY
◆ 8 : FULL STEREO TRACK

C VERSION

CD
⑤ : SPLIT TRACK/MELODY
⑥ : FULL STEREO TRACK

CONSTIPATED DUCK

BY JEFF BECK

C VERSION

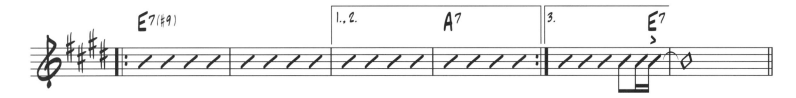

CD
◆ 9 : SPLIT TRACK/MELODY
◆ 10 : FULL STEREO TRACK

GOODBYE PORK PIE HAT

BY CHARLES MINGUS

C VERSION

LED BOOTS

BY MAX MIDDLETON

C VERSION

CD

| 15 : SPLIT TRACK/MELODY |
| 16 : FULL STEREO TRACK |

C VERSION

SHE'S A WOMAN

WORDS AND MUSIC BY JOHN LENNON
AND PAUL McCARTNEY

MEDIUM REGGAE

SOLOS (3 CHORUSES)

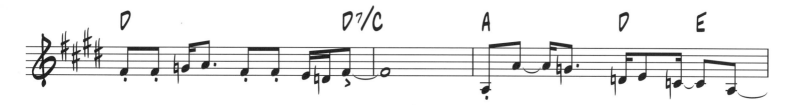

SOPHIE

BY NARADA MICHAEL WALDEN

C VERSION

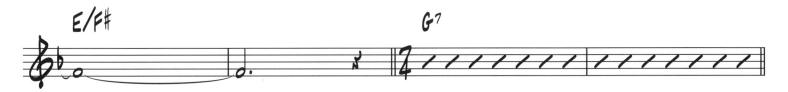

SOLOS (3 CHORUSES)

YOU KNOW WHAT I MEAN

CD

: SPLIT TRACK/MELODY
: FULL STEREO TRACK

BY JEFF BECK
AND MAX MIDDLETON

C VERSION

MEDIUM FUSION

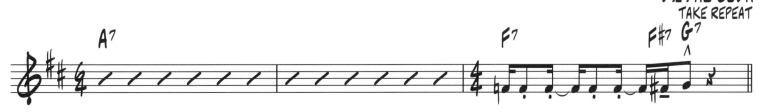

CD

◆13◆ : SPLIT TRACK/MELODY
◆14◆ : FULL STEREO TRACK

SCATTERBRAIN

BY JEFF BECK
AND MAX MIDDLETON

C VERSION

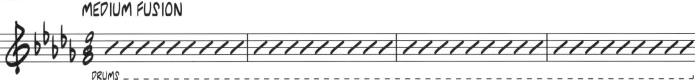

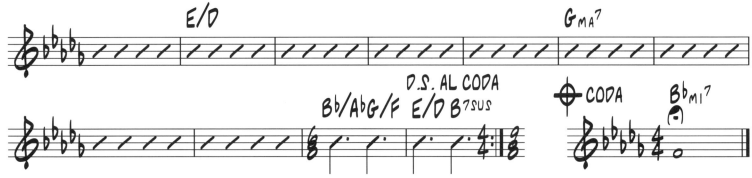

Cause We've Ended As Lovers

WORDS AND MUSIC BY
STEVIE WONDER

CD

3 : SPLIT TRACK/MELODY
4 : FULL STEREO TRACK

Bb VERSION

SLOW ROCK BALLAD

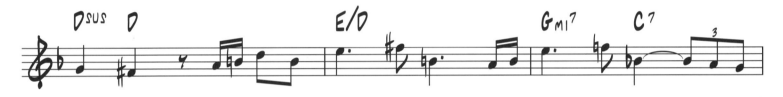

CD

① : SPLIT TRACK/MELODY
② : FULL STEREO TRACK

Blue Wind

BY JAN HAMMER

Bb VERSION

MEDIUM ROCK

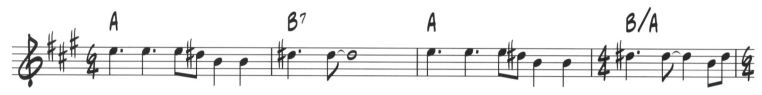

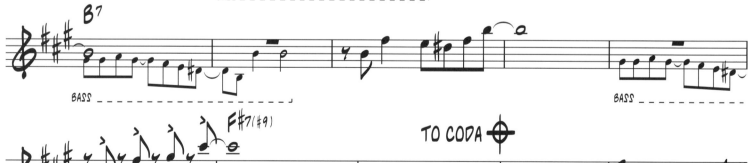

TO CODA ⊕

SOLOS (3 CHORUSES)

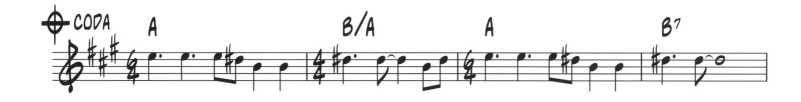

CONSTIPATED DUCK

BY JEFF BECK

Bb VERSION

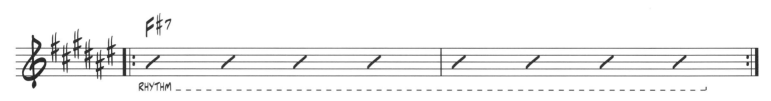

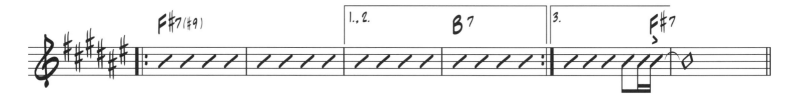

Freeway Jam

BY MAX MIDDLETON

GOODBYE PORK PIE HAT

CD
9 : SPLIT TRACK/MELODY
10 : FULL STEREO TRACK

BY CHARLES MINGUS

Bb Version

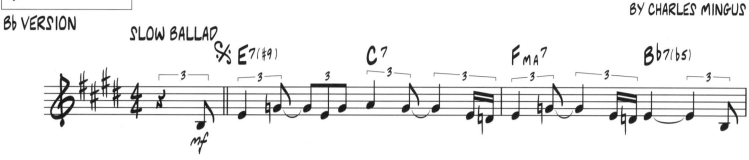

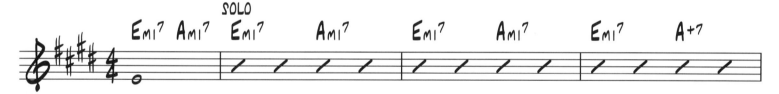

CD

LED BOOTS

BY MAX MIDDLETON

Bb VERSION

SCATTERBRAIN

BY JEFF BECK
AND MAX MIDDLETON

CD

13 : SPLIT TRACK/MELODY
14 : FULL STEREO TRACK

Bb VERSION

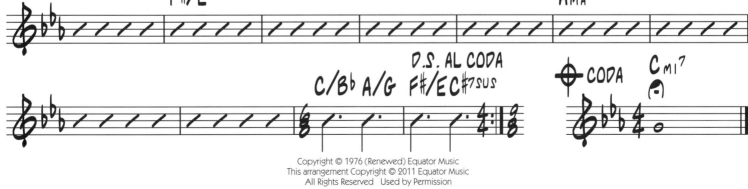

CD

15 : SPLIT TRACK/MELODY
16 : FULL STEREO TRACK

Bb VERSION

SHE'S A WOMAN

WORDS AND MUSIC BY JOHN LENNON
AND PAUL McCARTNEY

MEDIUM REGGAE

SOLOS (3 CHORUSES)

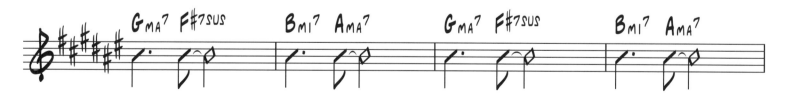

SOPHIE

BY NARADA MICHAEL WALDEN

CD
17 : SPLIT TRACK/MELODY
18 : FULL STEREO TRACK

Bb VERSION

SOLOS (3 CHORUSES)

YOU KNOW WHAT I MEAN

BY JEFF BECK
AND MAX MIDDLETON

Bb VERSION

MEDIUM FUSION

GUITAR - - - - - - -

(ADD PIANO/BASS)

BLUE WIND

BY JAN HAMMER

E♭ VERSION

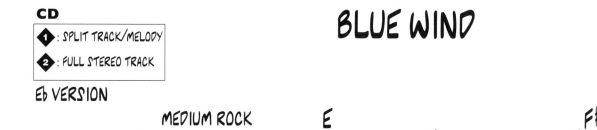

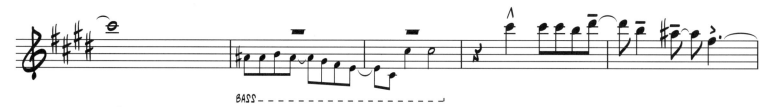

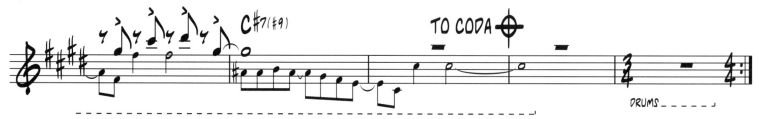

CD
◆3 : SPLIT TRACK/MELODY
◆4 : FULL STEREO TRACK

Cause We've Ended As Lovers

WORDS AND MUSIC BY
STEVIE WONDER

Eb VERSION

Freeway Jam

BY MAX MIDDLETON

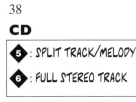

CONSTIPATED DUCK

BY JEFF BECK

Eb VERSION

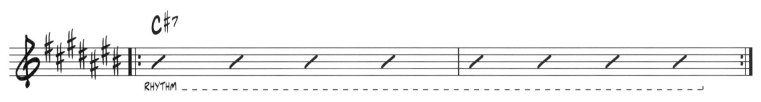

CD

9 : SPLIT TRACK/MELODY
10 : FULL STEREO TRACK

GOODBYE PORK PIE HAT

BY CHARLES MINGUS

Eb VERSION

SLOW BALLAD

LED BOOTS

BY MAX MIDDLETON

CD
11 : SPLIT TRACK/MELODY
12 : FULL STEREO TRACK

Eb VERSION

SHE'S A WOMAN

WORDS AND MUSIC BY JOHN LENNON
AND PAUL MCCARTNEY

Eb VERSION

SOLOS (3 CHORUSES)

CD

17 : SPLIT TRACK/MELODY
18 : FULL STEREO TRACK

SOPHIE

BY NARADA MICHAEL WALDEN

Eb VERSION

SOLOS (3 CHORUSES)

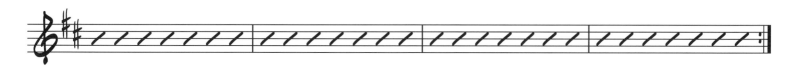

YOU KNOW WHAT I MEAN

BY JEFF BECK
AND MAX MIDDLETON

Eb VERSION

MEDIUM FUSION

GUITAR

(ADD PIANO/BASS)

mf

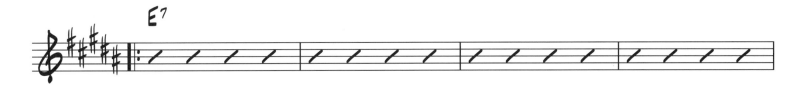

CD

13 : SPLIT TRACK/MELODY
14 : FULL STEREO TRACK

SCATTERBRAIN

BY JEFF BECK
AND MAX MIDDLETON

CAUSE WE'VE ENDED AS LOVERS

WORDS AND MUSIC BY
STEVIE WONDER

𝄢: C VERSION

CD

1 : SPLIT TRACK/MELODY
2 : FULL STEREO TRACK

BLUE WIND

BY JAN HAMMER

𝄢: C VERSION

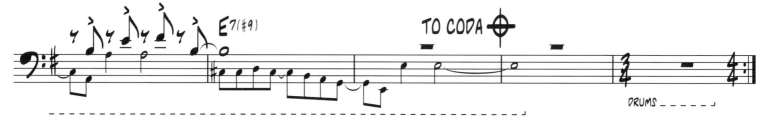

CD

5 : SPLIT TRACK/MELODY
6 : FULL STEREO TRACK

CONSTIPATED DUCK

BY JEFF BECK

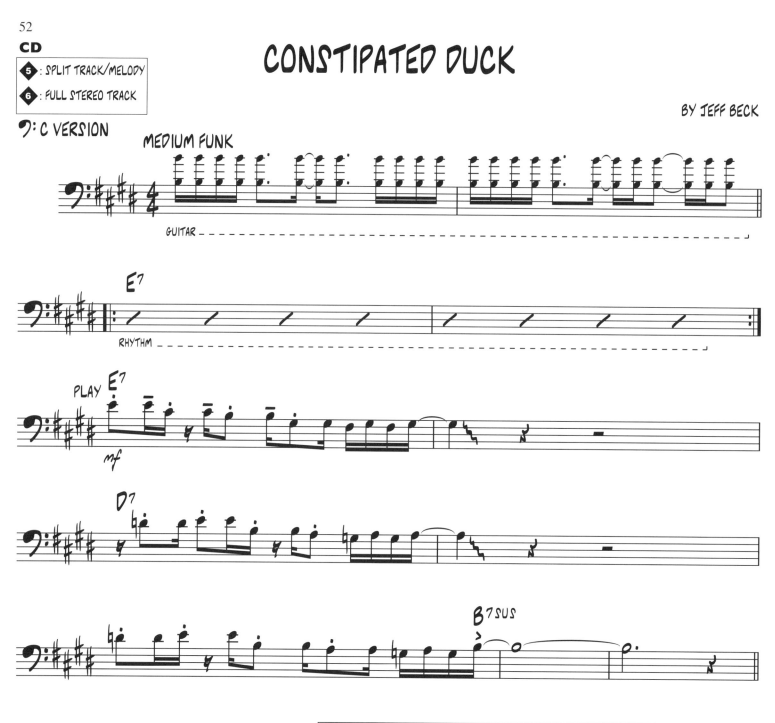

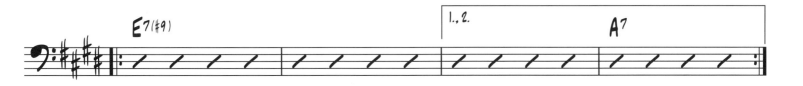

Freeway Jam

BY MAX MIDDLETON

GOODBYE PORK PIE HAT

BY CHARLES MINGUS

♪: C VERSION

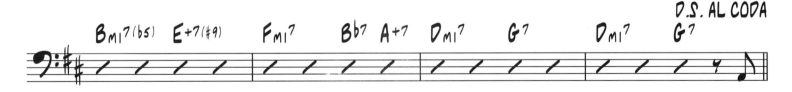

CD

11 : SPLIT TRACK/MELODY
12 : FULL STEREO TRACK

LED BOOTS

BY MAX MIDDLETON

SCATTERBRAIN

BY JEFF BECK
AND MAX MIDDLETON

𝄢 C VERSION

SHE'S A WOMAN

WORDS AND MUSIC BY JOHN LENNON
AND PAUL McCARTNEY

𝄢: C VERSION

MEDIUM REGGAE

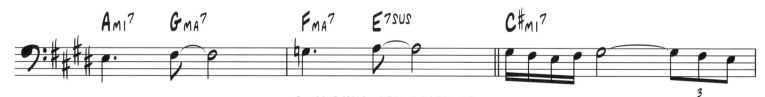

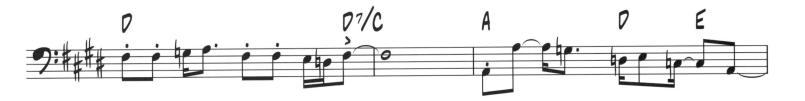

Sophie

BY NARADA MICHAEL WALDEN

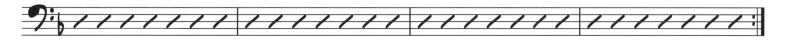

SOLOS (3 CHORUSES)

YOU KNOW WHAT I MEAN

𝄢: C VERSION

BY JEFF BECK
AND MAX MIDDLETON

MEDIUM FUSION

GUITAR -

(ADD PIANO/BASS)

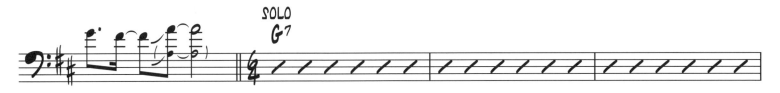

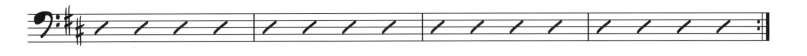

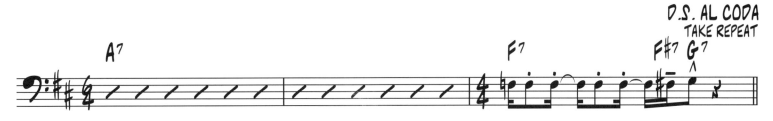

Presenting the Hal Leonard JAZZ PLAY-ALONG® SERIES

1. DUKE ELLINGTON
00841644 .... $16.95

1A. MAIDEN VOYAGE/ALL BLUES
00841158 .... $15.99

2. MILES DAVIS
00841645 .... $16.95

3. THE BLUES
00841646 .... $16.99

4. JAZZ BALLADS
00841691 .... $16.99

5. BEST OF BEBOP
00841689 .... $16.99

6. JAZZ CLASSICS WITH EASY CHANGES
00841690 .... $16.99

7. ESSENTIAL JAZZ STANDARDS
00843000 .... $16.99

8. ANTONIO CARLOS JOBIM AND THE ART OF THE BOSSA NOVA
00843001 .... $16.95

9. DIZZY GILLESPIE
00843002 .... $16.99

10. DISNEY CLASSICS
00843003 .... $16.99

11. RODGERS AND HART – FAVORITES
00843004 .... $16.99

12. ESSENTIAL JAZZ CLASSICS
00843005 .... $16.99

13. JOHN COLTRANE
00843006 .... $16.95

14. IRVING BERLIN
00843007 .... $15.99

15. RODGERS & HAMMERSTEIN
00843008 .... $15.99

16. COLE PORTER
00843009 .... $15.95

17. COUNT BASIE
00843010 .... $16.95

18. HAROLD ARLEN
00843011 .... $15.95

19. COOL JAZZ
00843012 .... $15.95

20. CHRISTMAS CAROLS
00843080 .... $14.95

21. RODGERS AND HART – CLASSICS
00843014 .... $14.95

22. WAYNE SHORTER
00843015 .... $16.95

23. LATIN JAZZ
00843016 .... $16.95

24. EARLY JAZZ STANDARDS
00843017 .... $14.95

25. CHRISTMAS JAZZ
00843018 .... $16.95

26. CHARLIE PARKER
00843019 .... $16.95

27. GREAT JAZZ STANDARDS
00843020 .... $15.99

28. BIG BAND ERA
00843021 .... $15.99

29. LENNON AND McCARTNEY
00843022 .... $16.95

30. BLUES' BEST
00843023 .... $15.99

31. JAZZ IN THREE
00843024 .... $15.99

32. BEST OF SWING
00843025 .... $15.99

33. SONNY ROLLINS
00843029 .... $15.95

34. ALL TIME STANDARDS
00843030 .... $15.99

35. BLUESY JAZZ
00843031 .... $15.99

36. HORACE SILVER
00843032 .... $16.99

37. BILL EVANS
00843033 .... $16.95

38. YULETIDE JAZZ
00843034 .... $16.95

39. "ALL THE THINGS YOU ARE" & MORE JEROME KERN SONGS
00843035 .... $15.99

40. BOSSA NOVA
00843036 .... $15.99

41. CLASSIC DUKE ELLINGTON
00843037 .... $16.99

42. GERRY MULLIGAN – FAVORITES
00843038 .... $16.99

43. GERRY MULLIGAN – CLASSICS
00843039 .... $16.95

44. OLIVER NELSON
00843040 .... $16.95

45. JAZZ AT THE MOVIES
00843041 .... $15.99

46. BROADWAY JAZZ STANDARDS
00843042 .... $15.99

47. CLASSIC JAZZ BALLADS
00843043 .... $15.99

48. BEBOP CLASSICS
00843044 .... $16.99

49. MILES DAVIS – STANDARDS
00843045 .... $16.95

50. GREAT JAZZ CLASSICS
00843046 .... $15.99

51. UP-TEMPO JAZZ
00843047 .... $15.99

52. STEVIE WONDER
00843048 .... $15.95

53. RHYTHM CHANGES
00843049 .... $15.99

54. "MOONLIGHT IN VERMONT" & OTHER GREAT STANDARDS
00843050 .... $15.99

55. BENNY GOLSON
00843052 .... $15.95

56. "GEORGIA ON MY MIND" & OTHER SONGS BY HOAGY CARMICHAEL
00843056 .... $15.99

57. VINCE GUARALDI
00843057 .... $16.99

58. MORE LENNON AND McCARTNEY
00843059 .... $15.99

59. SOUL JAZZ
00843060 .... $15.99

60. DEXTER GORDON
00843061 .... $15.95

61. MONGO SANTAMARIA
00843062 .... $15.95

62. JAZZ-ROCK FUSION
00843063 .... $14.95

63. CLASSICAL JAZZ
00843064 .... $14.95

64. TV TUNES
00843065 .... $14.95

65. SMOOTH JAZZ
00843066 .... $16.99

66. A CHARLIE BROWN CHRISTMAS
00843067 .... $16.99

67. CHICK COREA
00843068 .... $15.95

68. CHARLES MINGUS
00843069 .... $16.95

69. CLASSIC JAZZ
00843071 .... $15.99

70. THE DOORS
00843072 .... $14.95

71. COLE PORTER CLASSICS
00843073 .... $14.95

72. CLASSIC JAZZ BALLADS
00843074 .... $15.99

73. JAZZ/BLUES
00843075 .... $14.95

74. BEST JAZZ CLASSICS
00843076 .... $15.99

75. PAUL DESMOND
00843077 .... $14.95

76. BROADWAY JAZZ BALLADS
00843078 .... $15.99

77. JAZZ ON BROADWAY
00843079 .... $15.99

78. STEELY DAN
00843070 .... $14.99

79. MILES DAVIS – CLASSICS
00843081 .... $15.99

80. JIMI HENDRIX
00843083 .... $15.99

81. FRANK SINATRA – CLASSICS
00843084 .... $15.99

82. FRANK SINATRA – STANDARDS
00843085 .... $15.99

83. ANDREW LLOYD WEBBER
00843104 .... $14.95

84. BOSSA NOVA CLASSICS
00843105 .... $14.95

85. MOTOWN HITS
00843109 .... $14.95

86. BENNY GOODMAN
00843110 .... $14.95

87. DIXIELAND
00843111 .... $14.95

88. DUKE ELLINGTON FAVORITES
00843112 .... $14.95

89. IRVING BERLIN FAVORITES
00843113 .... $14.95

90. THELONIOUS MONK CLASSICS
00841262 .... $16.99

91. THELONIOUS MONK FAVORITES
00841263 .... $16.99

92. LEONARD BERNSTEIN
00450134 .... $15.99

93. DISNEY FAVORITES
00843142 .... $14.99

94. RAY
00843143 .... $14.99

95. JAZZ AT THE LOUNGE
00843144 .... $14.99

96. LATIN JAZZ STANDARDS
00843145 .... $14.99

97. MAYBE I'M AMAZED
00843148 .... $15.99

98. DAVE FRISHBERG
00843149 .... $15.99

99. SWINGING STANDARDS
00843150 .... $14.99

100. LOUIS ARMSTRONG
00740423 .... $15.99

101. BUD POWELL
00843152 .... $14.99

102. JAZZ POP
00843153 .... $14.99

103. ON GREEN DOLPHIN STREET & OTHER JAZZ CLASSICS
00843154 .... $14.99

104. ELTON JOHN
00843155 .... $14.99

105. SOULFUL JAZZ
00843151 .... $15.99

106. SLO' JAZZ
00843117 .... $14.99

107. MOTOWN CLASSICS
00843116 .... $14.99

108. JAZZ WALTZ
00843159 .... $15.99

109. OSCAR PETERSON
00843160 .... $15.99

110. JUST STANDARDS
00843161 .... $15.99

111. COOL CHRISTMAS
00843162 .... $15.99

114. MODERN JAZZ QUARTET FAVORITES
00843163 .... $15.99

115. THE SOUND OF MUSIC
00843164 .... $15.99

116. JACO PASTORIUS
00843165 .... $15.99

117. ANTONIO CARLOS JOBIM – MORE HITS
00843166 .... $15.99

118. BIG JAZZ STANDARDS COLLECTION
00843167 .... $27.50

119. JELLY ROLL MORTON
00843168 .... $15.99

120. J.S. BACH
00843169 .... $15.99

121. DJANGO REINHARDT
00843170 .... $15.99

122. PAUL SIMON
00843182 .... $16.99

123. BACHARACH & DAVID
00843185 .... $15.99

124. JAZZ-ROCK HORN HITS
00843186 .... $15.99

126. COUNT BASIE CLASSICS
00843157 .... $15.99

Prices, contents, and availability subject to change without notice.

FOR MORE INFORMATION, SEE YOUR LOCAL MUSIC DEALER, OR WRITE TO:

HAL•LEONARD®
CORPORATION
7777 W. BLUEMOUND RD. P.O. BOX 13819
MILWAUKEE, WISCONSIN 53213

Visit Hal Leonard online at
www.halleonard.com
for complete songlists.

0910